KIM JONG IL

OUR SOCIALISM CENTERED ON THE MASSES SHALL NOT PERISH

Talk to the Senior Officials of the
Central Committee of the Workers'
Party of Korea
May 5, 1991

University Press of the Pacific
Honolulu, Hawaii

Our Socialism Centered On the Masses Shall Not
Perish

by
Kim Jong Il

ISBN: 1-4102-0745-5

Copyright © 2003 by University Press of the Pacific

Reprinted from the 1991 edition

University Press of the Pacific
Honolulu, Hawaii
http://www.universitypressofthepacific.com

The popular masses have an age-long desire to enjoy an independent and creative life to the full in a society which is free from exploitation and oppression. In order to realize this desire, they have struggled, shedding their blood, against their oppressors. They have established a socialist society by overcoming all the trials that faced them. Socialism is a new social system which differs fundamentally from all the exploitative societies that have existed in human history. As such, it has to blaze a trail despite fierce struggles against the class enemies. Therefore, it may meet with transient setbacks in its progress. However, mankind's advance along the road of socialism is a law of historical development, and no force can ever check it.

Socialism, which has been established to meet the people's desire for independence and the requirements of the times, derives its unconquerable might from the masses' support for it and their confidence in it. Our people's support for and confidence in socialism are unshakable. Through their own lives they have experienced how precious the socialist system is. Throughout the decades of building socialism in our country there has never been any political instability or any wavering. Today the imperialists and reactionaries are working viciously to wipe out socialism, but our socialism continues to advance boldly along the path it has taken, without being swayed in the least by the enemy's dastardly attacks and slander. The progressive people of the world admire the durability and indestructibility of our socialism.

The secret of its durability and indestructibility is that it is centred upon the popular masses, that it has made the masses the genuine masters of society and that it has devoted

1

everything to the service of the masses. Because our socialism serves the popular masses, our people regard socialism as the cradle of their lives and of their happiness, and they entrust their destiny entirely to socialism. Our people, who are enjoying unlimited happiness and a genuine life in a socialist society under the wise leadership of the Party and the leader, are working with devotion to safeguard the socialist system and accomplish the socialist cause.

1

Socialism in our country is the socialism of our own style; it is the application of the great Juche idea and is centred upon the popular masses.

The great leader Comrade Kim Il Sung, in founding the Juche idea many years ago, reflected the aspirations of the masses and the requirements of the times. He has thus provided our age, the age of independence, with a new guiding ideology.

The Juche idea is a man-centred outlook on the world. It has clarified the essential qualities of man as a social being with independence, creativity and consciousness. It has, on this basis, evolved the new philosophical principle that man is the master of everything and decides everything. The Juche idea has established the viewpoint and attitude of dealing with everything in man's interests and approaching all changes and developments on the basis of man's activities. The Juche idea has raised man's dignity and value to the highest level. Because it is the embodiment of the Juche idea, our socialism is a man-centred socialism under which man is the master of everything and everything serves him.

By man, whom it regards as the master of everything and as the most precious and the most powerful being, the Juche idea means the working masses. The Juche idea views the popular masses as the driving force of social movement. The social movement is started and developed by the independent, creative and conscious activities of the people, its driving force. Without the participation of the popular masses, no social movement for the transformation of nature and society can take place, nor can socio-historical progress be made. The popular masses are the driving force of social movement because they create everything in society and, through their struggle, ensure the progress of history. Although they promote the social movement and make history, they cannot occupy the position of masters in all societies. In an exploitative society, the exploiting class that eats the bread of idleness, not the history-making masses, is king. A socialist society is one that puts an end to the society in which the position of master is inverted; it makes the popular masses the genuine masters. Our socialism is centred upon the popular masses in that it makes them the masters of everything, commensurate with their position and role in socio-historical progress, and makes everything serve them.

Our socialism for the masses meets the aspirations and desires of the working class most thoroughly. The Juche idea is the revolutionary ideology of the working class, and it represents the desires of the working class. It identifies the working class as the core of the driving force of the revolution. The working class embodies in itself at the highest level man's intrinsic desire to live and develop independently and creatively. It requires that man leads an independent and creative life, free from all manner of enslavement and bondage. It has the historical mission of emancipating not only itself but all the members of society from every form of enslavement and bondage and bringing complete independence to the popular masses.

In former days our country was a backward colonial, semi-feudal society, and so the working class was not large, yet it was the strongest in the spirit of independence and revolution. As this advanced class, it constituted the core of the revolutionary forces. Ever since the anti-imperialist, anti-feudal democratic revolution, the great leader has held up the working class as the leading revolutionary class and has made its class requirements and national requirements the starting-point of all his revolutionary lines and policies. In our country all the revolutions—the anti-imperialist national-liberation revolution, the anti-feudal democratic revolution, the social-ist revolution and the building of socialism—have been carried out successfully under the leadership of the working class. Our working class has grown steadily in strength, its role has increased and it is now successfully assimilating the whole of society to itself. With its gradual transformation on the pattern of the working class, the general appearance of our socialist society is being perfected as a society assimilated to the working class, as a classless society.

When I say that our socialism meets the intrinsic desire of the working class, I do not mean that our socialist society exists only for the working class. The requirements of the working class agree with those of all the other classes and sections that are interested in social progress; the society that satisfies the requirements of the working class also meets the requirements of other classes and sections. The Juche idea has defined as the components of the driving force of the revolution not only the working class but also the peasantry, the intelligentsia and other broad sections of the population, and advocates that their interests, too, should be met.

The peasantry, along with the working class, constitutes the major component of the driving force of the revolution; it is the motive force of the revolution. In former days when the peasantry accounted for the majority of the population in our country, it was always an important matter in the revolution to meet the interests of the peasants in full. In regarding the peasantry, along with the working class, as the main revolutionary force, the great leader saw to it that all the problems arising in the revolution were solved to meet the requirements of the peasantry, as well as those of the working class. Under the wise guidance of the Party and the leader, the agrarian reform was carried out to meet the age-long desire of the peasants to own land, and the socialist revolution in the postwar years was accomplished on the principle of voluntary cooperation and in the original way of reorganizing the form of the rural economy on socialist lines prior to technical re-equipment; all this was in accordance with the desire of the peasantry. With a view to the ultimate realization of the desire of the farmers, the leader published the theses on the socialist rural question and has given energetic guidance to the struggle to implement these theses. Our Party's consistent policy in championing the farmers' interests is to ensure that the state and society help the farmers in every possible, responsible manner to realize their desires and requirements. In our country, as indicated by the theses on the socialist rural question, the working-class guidance of the farmers, industrial assistance to agriculture, and urban support for the rural communities are being stepped up in every way, and the cause of making agriculture industrial and modern and of assimilat-

5

ing the farmers to the working class is being realized with success.

Intellectuals play an important role in the revolution and construction, and their role is enhanced with social development. It is very important in the revolution and construction to deal with intellectuals properly. Ever since the first days of his revolutionary activities, the great leader has regarded intellectuals as a component of the driving force of the revolution, as a major revolutionary force, and has guided them to work for the revolution. In view of the fact that the old-line intellectuals, as colonial intellectuals, had the anti-imperialist spirit of independence and a democratic revolutionary spirit, our Party trusted them without hesitation, re-educated them and guided them to work for the working class. It has also trained a large number of new intellectuals of worker and peasant origin and thus built up an army of intellectuals. Under the wise leadership of the Party and the leader, our intellectuals are making an active contribution to the cause of socialism and communism by displaying all their revolutionary enthusiasm and creative talents in all fields of the revolution and construction.

The exploiting class is not the driving force of social movement; it is a reactionary force and the target of the revolution. Dealing with the working masses as the driving force of the revolution and viewing the exploiting class as the target of the revolution on no account mean that people's standpoint and attitude towards the revolution and counter-revolution should be defined merely on the basis of their social class. People's social class influences their actions, but it does so through their ideological consciousness. Even people of an undesirable class origin, if under a revolutionary influence, can contribute to the revolution. The Juche idea's approach towards people of different classes and strata is that they should be judged by their ideas and actions and that the people who help towards social progress and the revolution should be trusted as part of the driving force of the revolution, without their social class origin being questioned.

Our Party has never hesitated to trust all the people who have come out in the struggle for the masses' independence, and has guided them along the path of revolution. For the anti-imperialist, anti-feudal democratic revolution in our country, our Party formed a revolutionary force of not only the major classes, but also conscientious national capitalists, honest men of religion and all other forces that were opposed to imperialism and aspired to democracy. In the socialist revolution, it did not eliminate rich peasants and capitalist businessmen and entrepreneurs; it admitted them into the cooperative economy on the principle of voluntary participation and led them to be transformed into socialist working people. Our Party has been leading all these transformed people to socialism and communism by trusting them as its lasting companions, rather than as temporary fellow travellers, no matter which class or stratum they came from.

Our socialism has been able to grow stronger and develop steadily, enjoying the unqualified support and confidence of the popular masses, because our Party has strengthened the driving force of the revolution and has built our socialism on the most durable and broadest foundation of social classes by promptly frustrating the counter-revolutionary schemes of a handful of hostile forces on the strength of its just class and mass line, at the same time as rallying different sections of the broad masses behind itself and the Government of the Republic.

The members of a social collective are bound together by

both the interests of the collective and those of individuals. The manner of combining these two categories of interests is an important factor that determines the progressive character of the social system. A capitalist society is ruled by egoism which sets the interests of the community against those of individuals and places the interests of individuals above those of the community. Egoism inevitably results in social inequality and "an increasing imbalance between rich and poor", and it produces conflicting relations among people. Egoism conflicts with the intrinsic nature of man as a social being. Because he is a social being capable of shaping his destiny only within the social community, man has an intrinsic need for collectivism. The Juche idea has made clear that the masses, and not an individual, are the driving force of the revolution and that collectivism, and not egoism, is an intrinsic requirement of man. The basic requirement of collectivism is that the interests of the collective should be placed above those of individuals, that the two types of interests should be harmonized and that the interests of individuals should be realized through the realization of those of the collective. That which is contrary to collectivism is not the individual interests themselves but egoism which seeks to satisfy only individual interests at the expense of collective interests. In our socialist society, which is the application of the man-centred Juche idea, the interests of every individual are respected, and the maximum social benefits and consideration are accorded to every member of the society, on the basis of protecting the interests of the collective thoroughly, and the relationship of the unity and cooperation of the whole society is fully mature.

A country and nation is the most comprehensive of social communities. It is a solid organization of people, a body with a common destiny, that has been formed socially and historically. The revolution and construction are conducted with the country and nation as a unit, and the interests of the social collective and those of the popular masses are realized within the unit of the country and nation. Outside the country and nation the popular masses cannot realize their desire for independence. The Juche idea regards the safeguarding of the independence of the country and nation as a fundamental requirement for realizing the masses' independence. When the imperialists are working viciously to trample upon the sovereignty of the country and nation, the thorough safe-guarding of its independence is vital to meeting the masses' desire for independence and their interests.

With the clear understanding that independence is the lifeblood of the country and nation, our Party and our people have always made it their cardinal task to safeguard the independence of their country and nation in their struggle for the revolution and construction. As a result, we have been able to build a dignified and powerful socialist country which is independent, self-sufficient, and self-reliant in its defence; we have been able to continue our dynamic advance along the revolutionary road by foiling the now-worsening anti-socialist moves of the imperialists and reactionaries.

The struggle to champion the interests of the country and nation and to realize its independence is linked with the worldwide struggle for independence. Realizing worldwide independence by opposing the domination and subjugation of one country and nation by another and inequality among nations is a major requirement of the Juche idea which advocates independence. The cause of realizing independence throughout the world requires, as essential, friendship and cooperation among countries and nations. Strengthening cooperation among all countries and nations, large and small, on the principles of independence, equality and mutual respect creates favourable conditions for the people to realize their independence. At a time when the allied imperialist forces are resorting to evil schemes to trample upon the independence of the popular masses, it is very important to strengthen anti-imperialist international solidarity. All countries and all nations that advocate independence must unite solidly and struggle jointly under the revolutionary banner of anti-imperialist independence. Only then will they be able to frustrate the imperialists' schemes of intervention and aggression and succeed in achieving independence throughout the world.

Our people, guided by the ideals of independence, peace and friendship, have been strengthening international solidarity and developing the relations of friendship and cooperation with the peoples of all countries who aspire to independence; they have been effecting multilateral exchange with all the countries that are friendly towards ours, on the principles of equality and mutual benefit. In spite of the difficult conditions in which they are conducting the revolution and construction in direct confrontation with the US imperialists, our people have been giving unstinted material and moral support and encouragement to the peoples of the third world who are struggling for independence.

Being the application of the Juche idea, the revolutionary idea of the era of independence, our socialism is the best socialism; it is centred upon the masses and strongly champions the desire of the working class and other social strata, the nation's right to independence and the aspirations of the world's people to independence.

Socialism is a cause for the popular masses, and socialism

and the interests of the masses can never be separated. In order to safeguard the interests of the masses, we must be faithful to the cause of socialism, and in order to champion the cause of socialism, we must thoroughly safeguard the interests of the masses. The aspirations and demands of the popular masses are the criterion for judging the truth of all social phenomena and the guide to all revolutionary activities. In future, too, we must at all times attach prime importance to the interests of the masses in the revolution and construction and deal with everything to meet them. We must firmly maintain the principle of thoroughly defending the fundamental interests of the popular masses and meeting their immediate interests by closely combining the two.

In order to build socialism that is centred on the popular masses, we must adhere to a revolutionary stand which enables the masses to maintain their position as the masters of the revolution and construction and play their role as such. No matter how much importance we may attach to the desires and interests of the masses, we shall be unable to meet them properly in practice if we do not maintain a correct stand in our efforts to meet them.

If the popular masses are to maintain their position as the masters of the revolution and construction and to play their role as such, they must adhere to the Juche stand, in other words, the stands of independence and creativity. The stands of independence and creativity are the fundamental stands which must be maintained in the revolution and construction.

The independent stand is the stand for the masses to maintain their independent position as the masters of the revolution and construction and of their own destiny; the basic requirement of this stand is for them to exercise their rights as the masters of the revolution and construction and fulfil their responsibilities as such. The independent stand is expressed in exercising the right to independence in all spheres of social life. If the popular masses are to exercise the right to independence, they must deal with all matters in the revolution and construction by their own decisions and judgements so as to meet their desires and interests. The right to independence is not provided by others. The popular masses must win their independence and defend it through their own struggle as the masters of their own destiny. If the masses are to maintain their position as the masters of their own destiny and safeguard their right to independence and their dignity, they must accept full responsibility for solving all problems on the principle of self-reliance.

The creative stand is the stand for the popular masses to fulfil their role as people who transform nature and society and shape their own destiny; the basic requirement of this stand is for them to believe in their own inexhaustible creative power and solve all problems creatively by relying on their own creativity. A social movement is a creative movement; it is the process of a struggle between the new and the old. The masses are creators; they overcome the old and create the new. History advances and the revolution is promoted on the strength of the inexhaustible creativity of the masses. In order to give a strong impetus to the revolution and construction, we must maintain the attitude of fostering the creativity of the masses and enhancing their creative role. The creative activities of the masses are always conducted in concrete subjective and objective conditions. The thoughts and feelings, as well as the preparedness, of the masses who create new things vary according to the countries they live in, and the socio-economic and material conditions under which the creative activities are conducted also differ from country to country. In the revolution and construction one must always adhere to the attitude of solving every problem to suit the specific situation in one's own country.

The practical experience we have gained in our revolution clearly shows that when the Juche stand is firmly maintained any problem, however complex and difficult, in the revolution and construction can be solved.

The socio-historical conditions of our revolution made it imperative to solve every problem from our own conviction to meet the will of our people and to suit the actual situation in our country. We started the revolution in a backward, colonial, semi-feudal society and had to build socialism under difficult circumstances in which the country was divided into the north and the south and everything was destroyed in the war. No ready-made formula capable of coping with such a situation could be found anywhere, still less one capable of blazing a trail in building socialism after the establishment of the socialist system. This required us to consider for ourselves all the problems raised in the revolution and construction and find solutions that suited the situation in our country.

From the Juche stand the great leader advanced original theories on the anti-imperialist national-liberation revolution, the anti-feudal democratic revolution and the socialist revolution, and he systematized them; he has perfected a new theory on the building of socialism and communism in a comprehensive manner. The theory and strategy and tactics on the revolution and construction the leader authored by implementing the Juche idea are a revolutionary theory centred on the working masses; they are the strategy and tactics of the revolution which are based on the role of the working masses. They are a perfect revolutionary theory of communism which encompasses a comprehensive system of the theory of national, class and man's emancipation and the theory of the transformation of society, nature and man. Because the original revolutionary theory and strategy and tactics evolved by the leader light up their way ahead, our people have been able to carry the cause of socialism along a straight path to victory without the slightest deviation.

The internal and external situation of our revolution was very complex; this made it vital for our people to promote the revolution and construction for themselves by fully displaying the revolutionary spirit of self-reliance. It is not easy for a small country to conduct the revolution and construction by itself. It was particularly arduous for our country to build socialism from scratch by its own efforts because the country was in sharp confrontation with a formidable imperialist foe and because it took over only backwardness, poverty and a devastated economy from the old society and the preceding age. However, our people did not undertake the revolution and construction with the help of anyone else. They were firmly convinced of their being the masters of their own destiny and of being capable of shaping their own destiny, and they formed a solid union behind the Party and the leader and hewed out the path of socialism, overcoming every trial by their own efforts.

Because it has adhered to the Juche stand in the revolution and construction, our Party has been able to uphold the dignity of the nation and revolutionary principles under all circumstances, however complicated, and firmly carry forward the cause of socialism. The prevailing complex situation requires that we should maintain the Juche stand still more firmly in the revolution and construction. With the imperialists and reactionaries resorting to vicious anti-socialist manoeuvres and directing the spearhead of their attack at those countries which maintain revolutionary principles, we must adhere to the Juche stand in the revolution and construction more firmly than ever before. We must be fully aware that adhering to this stand is vital to the destiny of the country and the nation, and consistently implement the Party's line and policy of independence, solving all problems to suit the situation in our country by drawing on the creativity of our people.

2

The socialism of our own style which is centred upon the masses and has been built by our own efforts to suit the situation in our country, in accordance with the line chosen by our people, is displaying great advantages and vitality.

Our socialist system is the best of all social systems, providing as it does an independent and creative life for the popular masses. Our people's desire to lead an independent and creative life to the full, free from every manner of enslavement and bondage, is being brilliantly realized in all aspects of their political, economic, ideological and cultural lives.

A political life is of decisive importance in a social life. Only when they participate in a political life as masters of the state and society can the popular masses lead an independent and creative life. In order to take part in a political life as masters, as masters of their destiny, the popular masses must have political power in their own hands.

Motivated by the Juche idea, the great leader a long time

ago proposed the original line of a people's government and led our people to build their government in accordance with their will. The people's government established by our people in accordance with their own will is a genuine people's government of which the working class and the broad working masses are the masters and which firmly champions the interests of the people.

In our country, where the people are the masters of the government, all the working people, as equal members of society, participate in all aspects of the exercising of state power and state administration with the attitude befitting masters and equal political rights, and they are freely conducting socio-political activities.

Our socialist society is a genuinely democratic society which fully provides the people with true political rights and freedom. By nature, socialism cannot be separated from democracy. Only socialist democracy is true democracy.

As long as there is a class struggle, democracy assumes a class character and is linked with dictatorship. Socialist democracy gives full scope to democracy for the popular masses, but it exercises dictatorship over the class enemies who infringe upon democracy. The fact that the imperialists and reactionaries slander socialist democracy because social- ist society exercises dictatorship over the class enemies means, in the final analysis, that they want us to open the way for their criminal moves against socialism. When the imperialists and their stooges commit subversive acts and sabotage against socialist democracy, it is only natural that sanctions are applied against the class enemies who infringe upon the independence of the popular masses. The bourgeois de- mocracy which the imperialists and reactionaries try to force upon other people is anti-popular "democracy" which allows

16

a handful of exploiting class members to exercise the full scope of democracy and dictatorship over the working masses. Bourgeois democracy, which harshly suppresses the struggle of the broad working masses for democratic freedom and the right to survive, can never be true democracy. The imperialists and reactionaries are advertising the bourgeois parliamentary system and the bourgeois multi-party system as "democracy". However, in such systems big monopolists are the real behind-the-scenes manipulators of politics. When they find even the formal parliamentary system or the multi-party system to be an obstacle to their reactionary rule, the imperialists and reactionaries immediately overthrow it and resort to overt fascist rule. There is clear historical evidence of this.

The popular character of socialist democracy and the anti-popular character of bourgeois democracy are manifest with regard to human rights. In our socialist society, which regards man as most precious, human rights are fully guaranteed by law; not the slightest practice infringing upon them is tolerated. In our country full rights for the people, ranging from the rights to employment, food, clothing and housing to the rights to education and medical care, are guaranteed. No other such country can be found in the world. The imperialists and reactionaries, posing as the "champions of human rights", are now vilifying socialism, but it is they alone who are violating human rights. The imperialists and reactionaries who commit political terrorism against innocent people and social figures demanding freedom and democracy and who deprive the working people of their elementary democratic freedom and right to exist have no entitlement to talk about human rights. The violent attacks upon human rights perpetrated in south Korea at the instigation of the US imperialists clearly show how hypocritical and shameless the imperialists' professed "championing of human rights" is.

Socialist democracy is guaranteed by the observance of the socialist law. The observance of the socialist law is a democratic procedure, which fundamentally differs from the bourgeois legal procedure, which is a means of ruling the people by force. Socialist society is an organized society based on collectivism, and social organization is guaranteed at a high level by socialist law. People's democratic rights and freedom are ensured by socialist law and good social order. Unlike capitalist law, which is an anti-popular means for the reactionary ruling classes to rule, our socialist law reflects the will of the working masses and is abided by thanks to the high level of their consciousness. Our people, thanks to our most popular socialist legal code, are being provided by law with full democratic rights and freedom as the masters of the state and society.

In socialist society, democracy is combined with centralism. If everyone thinks of himself with no regard to centralism, the masses will fail to realize their desire for independence. Democratic government is precisely an undertaking to incorporate the desires of the masses into policies and embody them as the will of the masses. It is only when the state provides centralized leadership under the guidance of a working-class party that true democracy can be guaranteed. Ensuring the centralized leadership of the state is a natural requirement of a socialist society. In a socialist society, all the members of which are integrated into a socio-political organism and live by helping and leading one another forward, the state is responsible for the life of everyone. That the state takes the responsibility for looking after all the members of society is an intrinsic advantage of a socialist society over a capitalist society. In a capitalist society the people's lives are the concern of the individuals alone, and they are left to the mercy of spontaneity; the bourgeois state does not care at all if people starve to death. In a socialist society the state function of taking responsibility for everyone's life is performed by the centralized leadership.

The performance of centralized leadership by the socialist state is not merely an exercise of power. Of course, the socialist government exercises its power in conformity with its character, but the socialist government, the master of which is the people and which serves the people, must not consider itself as omnipotent. Only the government of the exploiting class which rules the people politically regards its power as absolute. The socialist government of our country is not merely a power organ, but a government which serves the people; it represents the working people's right to independence, organizes their creative ability and activity, is responsible as the national administrator for the people's lives and protects their interests. If the socialist state allows its function of centralized leadership, which is necessary for the performance of its mission and duty as the servant of the people, to weaken it cannot fulfil its responsibility to provide a livelihood for the people and, worse still, a state of anarchy may be created in the socialist society and socialism may be endangered. For the purpose of obliterating socialism, the people's enemy is, under the cloak of "democracy", working against the centralized leadership of the socialist state.

We must continue to strengthen the people's government, enhance its functions and role, establish more thoroughly the attitude of observing socialist law and the democratic way of life and thus give free rein to socialist democracy. By carrying out the Party's lines and policies and implementing the revolutionary mass line, our people's government organs must fulfil their mission and duty honourably as administrators responsible for the people's lives.

People participate in a political life in society through not only the government but also political parties and social organizations. If they are to become the genuine masters of politics, the masses of the people must not only be masters of the state power, but also lead a political life in parties and other organizations, as befitting masters. The importance and role of a political life in parties and social organizations become greater in a socialist society because a socialist society is a society in which the leader, the party and the masses make up a socio-political organism. In a socialist society, people can preserve their socio-political integrity and maintain close ties with the leader only when they lead a political life in a working-class party and the political organizations led by it. Our working people regard it as valuable to lead a political life in a Party and the political organizations led by it, and they participate willingly in their activities.

Democratic centralism is a principle of the organizational life of our Party and working people's organizations. In a politico-organizational life there is neither a superior nor a subordinate; everyone exercises his rights and performs his duties on an equal basis. Democratic suggestions made by Party members and the working people through their Party and working people's organizations are incorporated into Party and state policies, and it is on the strength of their creative initiative that these policies are carried out.

Party and working people's organizations form a school for educating and training Party members and the working people. Through their politico-organizational life Party members and the working people digest the leader's revolutionary ideas as their political pabulum, and they train themselves with the help of their organizations and comrades. In our country all Party members and all the working people are fully equipped with the Juche idea and, rallied rock-solid behind the Party and the leader, promote their valuable socio-political integrity; this would be totally inconceivable if they did not lead a revolutionary politico-organizational life.

The imperialists and reactionaries disparage a political life in a working-class party and other political organizations led by the party as if it were the "restraint" of freedom; they do so precisely because a politico-organizational life is an important source of the politico-ideological might of socialist society. If people in a socialist society do not lead a proper political life in a working-class party and other political organizations led by the party, they cannot preserve their socio-political integrity; worse still, they may go astray and ruin their socio-political integrity and even play into the hands of the reactionaries, being deceived by counter-revolutionaries. It is only when they lead a revolutionary politico-organizational life that they can play a part in implementing Party and state policies as befitting masters and live a worthwhile life. We must consolidate and develop our well-regulated politico-organizational system, encourage Party members and the working people to strengthen their spirit of leading a voluntary politico-organizational life and ensure that all the people promote their socio-political integrity.

An economic life constitutes the basis of a social life. The independent and creative life of people is guaranteed by a free and prosperous economic life.

Since the popular masses are the masters of their own destiny they must be the masters of their economic life.

Whether they become the masters of their economic life or not depends upon the economic system of the society, the system of ownership in particular. The popular masses create social wealth in the outmoded exploitative society, but they are not the masters of this wealth because they have been deprived of the means of production by a handful of members of the exploiting class. The popular masses who aspire to a new society free from exploitation and oppression desire, above all else, to own the means of production. This desire has become a reality in our country through the democratic and socialist revolutions. In our country the social ownership of the means of production holds undivided sway and, on the basis of this, the popular masses have become the genuine masters of their economic life and enjoy an independent and creative life.

The imperialists and reactionaries, loudly advertising the "advantages" of private ownership, are urging socialist countries to abandon social ownership and revert to private ownership, but the reactionary nature of the system of private ownership was proved a long time ago. The vaunted "advantages" of private ownership represent unbridled competition to rake in more money, competition based on the law of the jungle. This competition inevitably engenders exploitation and oppression and degrades the working people to the slaves of capital. Only in a socialist society which is based on social ownership can the popular masses enjoy an independent and creative life as the genuine masters of society. The people of our country have themselves experienced that social ownership alone provides them with a prosperous and cultured life; they hold the system very dear and strive with devotion to consolidate and develop it. The consolidation of social ownership is a law-governed requirement of the socialist society for it to develop. We must accomplish the historic task of establishing single all-people ownership by bringing cooperative ownership closer to all-people ownership while steadily enhancing the dominant role of the latter.

A socialist economy in which the popular masses own the means of production must be managed by the popular masses themselves. By establishing the Taean work system, the great leader provided the best form of economic management whereby the socialist economy is managed by the masses themselves. The Taean work system is a fully scientific form of communist economic management which embodies the revolutionary mass line. In this work system the mass line is implemented admirably through the collective guidance of the Party committee. The collective guidance of the Party committee renders it possible to prevent individuals from managing the economy in a subjective and arbitrary manner, to enlist the complete collective wisdom of the masses and to encourage them by political methods to fulfil their economic tasks. The guidance of the Party committee over economic work, a method evolved by our Party, is essentially a form of policy guidance, political guidance, and it precludes the Party from taking administrative work upon itself and from working by administrative methods. In accordance with the decision of the Party committee, the Party officials work among the people, which is political work, and the administrative and technical workers do economic and technical work. Thanks to the collective guidance of the Party committee, all economic work is carried out in accordance with the Party's policies, the opinions of the masses are reflected in the management of the economy, and the sense of responsibility of officials and the enthusiasm of the people are displayed at a high level in their performance of economic tasks. The superiority and vitality of the Taean work system have been clearly demonstrated in practice. We must continue to implement the Taean work system to the full so as to develop our socialist economy at a steady and high rate by drawing on the unfathomable creativity of the popular masses, and we must provide our people with a richer and more cultured life.

Creative labour occupies an important place in an economic life. Through his labour man creates the material and cultural wealth he needs in his life and, in the course of this, trains himself into a more powerful being. The right to labour is one of the basic rights a man should enjoy as the master of society, and how this right is guaranteed is an important factor defining the progressive character of the social system.

Our socialist society grants the working people the full right to labour. Our working people are provided by the state with stable jobs in accordance with their abilities and aptitudes. The word "unemployment" has no place in the vocabulary of our people. Only in our socialist society which treats man as the most precious being is this true. A capitalist society, which regards man as the object of exploitation and as a producer of surplus value, cannot provide the working people with stable jobs. Capitalists use unemployment as a lever for speed-up and for exploiting the labour force at a lower cost. In a capitalist society a large number of unemployed and semi-unemployed people wander the streets, and even employed people have the constant fear of being dismissed.

For creative labour to be a more worthwhile effort, the working people should be freed from backbreaking labour and provided with more cultured and hygienic working conditions. The more the productive forces of society develop, the greater is the possibility for providing improved working conditions. But how this possibility is implemented depends largely on the character of the social system. Our Party raised the technical revolution for freeing the working people from hard labour as a task of the continuous revolution to be performed after the socialist system was established, and is striving to carry it out. Under the wise leadership of the Party and the leader, the historic task of freeing the working people, who have been freed from exploitation and oppression, from backbreaking labour is being fulfilled with success in our country. We must continue in our country to strengthen this, the best socialist labour system, press on with the technical revolution until we eliminate hard and backbreaking labour once and for all and make our people's creative labour more worthwhile.

Providing people with an equitable and affluent material life is a major requirement of socialist economic life. An equitable and affluent life is guaranteed for the popular masses only by the popular policies of the working-class party and the socialist state.

Thanks to the popular policies of our Party and the Government of our Republic, all our people are provided by the state and society with all the practical conditions they need for adequate food, clothing and housing and enjoy an equally happy life. They are supplied by the state with provisions virtually free of charge and receive the benefits of free education, free medical care and all the conditions they need for adequate food, clothing and housing. Moreover, as a result of the abolition of taxation, this word has disappeared from their vocabulary. In our country the state takes responsible care of the old and disabled people and children who have no means of support. In our country preferential, social treatment is accorded to merited people, including veterans who have been disabled in the fight for the noble cause of the fatherland and the people, and the Party and the state take warm care of them. Our people receive many benefits from the Party and the state. The popular policies of our Party and the Government of the Republic are eloquent proof of the advantages of our socialist system which is centred upon the popular masses.

The "welfare policies" pursued in capitalist countries are fundamentally different from the popular policies of a socialist society. They are aimed at disguising the class contradictions in that society and at pacifying the resistance of the working masses. Even if the "welfare policies" are enforced, this is done only in name and cannot improve the life of the working people.

In our country the socialist principle of distribution according to the quantity and quality of work done has been put into effect and such economic levers as pricing are used to suit the transitional character of socialist society. Wages and prices are assessed on the principle of improving the standard of living of the people systematically and equitably, and differences in wage-scales are slight and are narrowed gradually. The prices of mass consumption goods are set low, and those of goods essential to children and students even lower.

Under the wise leadership and great consideration of the Party and the leader all the members of our society are equally prosperous, free from any worries about food, clothing and housing, and are leading a happy life helping and leading one another forward. This is a characteristic of the socialist material well-being our people enjoy. We must not only continue to adhere to the most advantageous popular policies by which the Party and the state take responsible care of the material well-being of the people but also develop them as socialist construction progresses.

Material guarantees for the people's economic life are secured by the development of the nation's productive forces.

The socialist system provides a broad avenue for the development of the productive forces. The socialist economy which serves the people is not a market economy but a planned economy; it is not a dependent but an independent economy. The market economy which is geared to money-making and the dependent economy which enriches foreign monopolists totally conflict with the interests of the popular masses; neither of them can develop as fast as the socialist economy that develops on a planned and independent basis. The imperialists and their mouthpieces claim that the developed capitalist countries owe their "material prosperity" to what they call the "advantages" of the capitalist economic system, but this is a lie that deceives nobody. The developed capitalist nations have long been taking the road of capitalism, but the socialist countries were once economically backward or colonial or semi-colonial countries. The capitalist countries have achieved "material prosperity" through the harsh exploitation of the working people and the colonial plunder of the people of the third world while the socialist countries have not allowed themselves to do so. The imperialists may make colonies of some backward countries and invent "material prosperity" for the purpose of using it in their confrontation with the socialist countries, but this type of dependent economy can never bring genuine prosperity to the working masses, no matter how developed it is. Only a socialist economy developing on a planned, independent and national basis can bring genuine prosperity and happiness to the working masses. Only by building a sound independent national economy which develops in a planned way is it possible to secure political independence, strengthen the material and technical foundations of socialism, improve the people's material prosperity and give rein to the advantages of the socialist system.

When the imperialists are working craftily to impose the capitalist market economy upon other countries and make inroads into their economies by using "economic cooperation" and "aid" as a bait, it is all the more important firmly to maintain the principle of building a socialist economy. Under the leadership of the Party our people have built a powerful, independent national economy by giving full scope to the advantages of the planned socialist economy. They are pushing ahead with socialist construction, in spite of all the economic blockades imposed upon them by the imperialists and any world economic upheaval. We must further increase the economic might of the country and continue to improve the material prosperity of the people by carrying through the Party's policy of unified and detailed planning as well as its line of building an independent national economy, and by effecting a continual upsurge in the building of the socialist economy. We must develop economic exchange and cooperation in every way on the principles of equality and mutual benefit with all countries that are friendly towards our country. But we must reject all the imperialists' attempts to make inroads into our economy.

An ideological and cultural life is an important aspect of a social life. Through their ideological and cultural life people develop their independent ideological consciousness and creative ability, satisfy a variety of their cultural and emotional needs and acquire noble mental and moral traits.

A major characteristic of an ideological and cultural life in socialist society is that the popular masses not only create mental and cultural wealth but also own it and enjoy a noble ideological and cultural life. Since the popular masses are the masters of a socialist society, the working-class party and its state must act responsibly to provide the people with the conditions they need to lead a sound and rich ideological and cultural life. In our country the Party and the state act responsibly to provide the people with the conditions they need to lead an ideological and cultural life. This is the best system, and it accords with the requirements and aspirations of the popular masses. It is a major characteristic of our socialist society.

Their ideological life, along with their political life, is very important to people in their social life. People's qualities are determined by their ideological consciousness, which plays a decisive role in all their activities. The confrontation between progress and reaction, revolution and counter-revolution, is always based on confrontation in the ideological field.

An ideological life in a socialist society is based on the revolutionary ideas of the working class, and our people's ideological life is based on the Juche idea, the perfect revolutionary ideology of the working class. In any society the ideological life assumes a class character. Ideological consciousness reflects the class interests and requirements of the people. No class in history has ever refrained from claiming its ideological rule in society. In a capitalist society imperialists and monopolists try to impose a corrupt reactionary bourgeois ideology on the society. But in a capitalist society, which is divided into classes and sections with conflicting interests, it is impossible for a single idea to maintain its complete sway over the society and, accordingly, it is inevitable that different ideas and trends exist. This state of affairs is painted by the imperialists and their mouthpieces as ideological "freedom". In a capitalist society, where the power of capital dominates everything, there can be no genuine ideological freedom. Monopoly capitalists seize most of the propaganda media, among them publishing and radio and television broadcasting, with the power of money and spread their reactionary ideas by force; they do not hesitate even to resort to an overt repression of thoughts which they recognize as a danger to themselves. This is the ideological "freedom" that has been much vaunted by the imperialists and their mouthpieces.

While suppressing by force of arms the spreading of the Juche idea among the south Korean people, the US imperialists and their stooges are saying that we have no ideological "freedom". By nature, ideas cannot be obliterated by coercion. In south Korea the ranks of adherents to the Juche idea are expanding in spite of the harsh repression by the US imperialists and their stooges. The suppression of ideas is perpetrated by those who, with no better idea, try to impose anti-popular thoughts upon other people. Our people have accepted the Juche idea, an excellent man-centred thought as their conviction, of their own accord, and from their vital need.

A socialist society naturally requires the undivided sway of the revolutionary idea of the working class. It is a law that a single idea is predominant in socialist society where the socio-economic foundations of outmoded thoughts have been eradicated and class antagonism eliminated. Of course, it is not easy for the revolutionary idea of the working class to hold undivided sway in a socialist society, this is because a socialist society still retains survivals of obsolete ideas and is subject to the ideological and cultural infiltration of imperialism. Although man's ideological consciousness is influenced by the socio-economic conditions, the establishment of a new socio-economic system does not automatically alter people's ideological consciousness. There can be no blank in a man's mind; he cannot help being affected by either the revolutionary idea of the working class or bourgeois thoughts. Particularly when the imperialists and other reactionaries are bent on their evil scheme of ideological and cultural penetration into socialist countries, the slightest slackening of ideological education may result in the wind of bourgeois liberalism blowing in. It is a stereotyped trick of imperialists to try to smuggle their ideas into othei countries, prior to undisguised aggression. We must foil all imperialist attempts to send the wind of bourgeois liberalism blowing into socialist countries for the purpose of undermining them ideologically.

In order to eliminate the remnants of outworn ideas in socialist societies and check the infiltration of every form of unsound ideology from the outside, we must train our people to be communist revolutionaries of the Juche type by conducting the ideological revolution vigorously. The ideological revolution to transform the ideological consciousness of the people is a law-governed requirement in the building of socialism and communism as well as the most important revolutionary task facing the working-class party after the establishment of the socialist system. It is only when all the members of society are freed from the shackles of every manner of obsolete idea and trained to be firm communist revolutionaries of the Juche type through the ideological revolution that the driving force of the revolution can be strengthened and the cause of socialism and communism can be accomplished creditably. By laying the main stress on the ideological revolution, our Party has given its members and the working people intensive ideological education in various forms—education in the principles of the Juche idea, in Party policy, in loyalty, in our revolutionary traditions, in class attitude, in collectivism and in socialist patriotism. In this way it has equipped them fully with its revolutionary ideology, the Juche idea, and is imbuing the whole society with this single ideology. Our working people are fully displaying the revolutionary spirit of working with devotion for the Party, their fellow people, society and their collective. This is the true nature of the ideological life of our people, and a sure guarantee for the victory of our revolution lies in the fact that the whole of society is ringing with a revolutionary tone in its ideological life. Giving priority to the ideological revolution of the three revolutions—ideological, technical and cultural—is the consistent policy of our Party. We will in the future, too, adhere to the principle of giving precedence to the ideological revolution, maintain the existing system of ideological education as well as its content and methods, and develop ideological education in depth to meet the requirements of the developing situation. By doing this, we will prepare our people better to be communist revolutionaries of the Juche type.

In providing an independent and creative life for the people it is important to meet their cultural requirements. Our socialist system of a cultural life is an advantageous system for satisfying their cultural requirements. In our socialist society the working people are growing to be powerful beings with creative ability and qualifications. In our country, the land of learning where all the people study, the whole society is becoming intellectual. In this country a universal eleven-year compulsory education system is in force and higher education is developed, so that the younger generation are being trained as good national cadres, as builders of socialism. Under a well-organized education system of studying while working the working people are cultivating their creative talents while they work. Under a well-established system of study, with excellent study facilities for the entire Party and the whole society, all our officials and working people are improving their political and practical qualifications steadily.

Our country has created a socialist national culture and the people enjoy a rich cultural and aesthetic life to the full. Our revolutionary and popular culture which is national in form and socialist in content has developed and blossomed, so that our country is renowned as a country of brilliant culture, and as a country of art.

In our socialist society the people have acquired the communist moral traits required of independent beings so that they live in harmony, with a high sense of revolutionary comradeship and of their obligations, as well as revolutionary conscience, helping and leading one another forward.

The sound and rich cultural life of our people is the most valuable and worthwhile of cultural lives. By continuing to conduct the cultural revolution energetically, we will continue to raise the cultural level of society and bring our people's sound and noble cultural life into fuller bloom.

3

Socialism in our country is invincible socialism based on the single-hearted unity of the leader, the Party and the masses.

The driving force of a socialist society is the popular masses themselves. But only when the popular masses are closely united behind the Party and the leader can they play their role as the independent driving force of the revolution and successfully carry out socialist construction.

A socialist society is an organized society based on collectivism. Therefore, it can never forge a path spontaneously. When a socialist society is guided by a correct guiding idea and a scientific strategy and tactics, and when the political awareness of the popular masses and their sense of organization are raised, it can fully display its advantages and be steadily consolidated and developed. Presenting to the popular masses a correct guiding idea and a scientific strategy and tactics, and ensuring that they become politically conscious and organize themselves, is done by an outstanding leader of the working class and the party.

The leader is the centre of unity and cohesion which ensures that the popular masses become politically conscious and organize themselves so that they are united into a political force, and he is the centre of leadership at the head of the revolutionary struggle of the popular masses, leading it to victory with his scientific theory and strategy and tactics. He is the great revolutionary leader who defends the independent demands and interests of the popular masses; he has an unusual gift of foresight, is all-powerful in the leadership art and noble in personal virtue, and leads the people wisely in their struggle.

When, in the days of national suffering, our people were buffeted by the waves of adversity, unable to find the way to take, they eagerly sought an outstanding leader. This desire was magnificently fulfilled when the great Comrade Kim Il Sung became our people's leader. With our people under the leadership of Comrade Kim Il Sung, the greatest leader they had acclaimed in their history of several thousand years, they were able to put an end to their prolonged history of suffering, create a new era of revolution and forge a victorious new history of socialism. The excellent people-centred socialism of our own style built in our country is a brilliant fruition of the tireless and energetic activities of the great leader and his wise guidance, the leader who boundlessly loves the people and has devoted his whole life to their interests.

The idea and theory and the policy put forward by the great leader are the full embodiment of the people's will and requirements. Our great leader has taught us that the popular masses are teachers. Not in his office, but in the midst of the populace, he discovered the truth of the Juche principles, put these principles in a systematic form, reflecting the people's aspirations, and on the basis of a review of the experience of the struggle waged by the popular masses for realizing independence, he moulded the Juche idea into a comprehensive system. He has always mixed with the popular masses in order to discover their will and demands, and, on this basis, he has put forward new lines and policies. The leader also presented the Juche method of farming by systematizing the experience of farmers, working among them, while giving on-the-spot guidance at many rural villages. The famous Chongsanri spirit and Chongsanri method which are the communist guiding idea and the method of guidance of mass leadership, were also presented by him by systematizing the aspirations and will of the farmers of Chongsan-ri while sharing board and lodging with them.

He has covered millions of miles in giving his on-the-spot guidance, and in the course of this he has put forward lines and policies reflecting the aspirations and will of the popular masses, and encouraged them to implement them, thus leading our revolution into an uninterrupted upsurge. The

35

Juche method of leadership which the great leader has created, personally setting a shining example, his method of work, has become our Party's traditional method of work.

The single-hearted unity of the leader, the Party and the masses which is an imperishable lifeblood of our socialism emanates from the great leader's infinite love for the people. Because the leader shows boundless affection for the people and meets all their desires, our people respect him profoundly as their true father, hold him in high esteem and are completely devoted to him.

The leader effects his guidance through the working-class party. The working-class party is the vanguard detachment made up of the leading elements of the working people, and it is the General Staff of the revolution leading the struggle for the independence of the popular masses.

The working-class party is the sole guiding force in socialist society. No other political organization can take its position and role. The government in power and working people's organizations, mass-based political organizations made up of certain sections of society, cannot take the place of the working-class party in view of their characters, and they should be subject to its guidance. Nor can political parties other than the working-class party become the guiding force in socialist society. Socialist society is a transitional society in which class distinctions and other differences remain. Therefore, other political parties can exist with the working-class party. But parties representing certain political forces or sections can never take the position and role of the working-class party. Transferring the hegemony in socialist society which embodies the demand of the working class to the hands of a political party other than the working-class party means, in the final analysis, abandoning socialism. Other political parties in a socialist society are not political organizations competing with the working-class party for power. They should be friendly political organizations cooperating with one another in conditions where the leadership of the working-class party over the whole society is ensured. This is an essential demand of a socialist society, where the desire for independence of the farmers, working intellectuals and other broad sections of the people, to say nothing of the working class, the leading class, is being met. If this demand is disregarded and the leading position and role of the working-class party are weakened or ignored, the working people will be reduced to unorganized masses bereft of their guiding centre and will finally break up. The result may be that counter-revolutionary elements mislead public opinion and seize power. Whether the leadership of the working-class party over a socialist society is ensured or not is a crucial problem affecting the destiny of socialism.

Our people regard the Workers' Party of Korea, their working-class party, as their only guiding force, entrust their destiny entirely to it and faithfully uphold its leadership.

The advantages and solidity of socialism depend on the revolutionary character of the working-class party, the guiding force of socialist society, and its leadership role.

Our Party is guided by the people-centred Juche idea and is fighting to fulfil the cause of independence for the popular masses. Regarding the people-centred Juche idea as its only guiding ideology and the complete realization of their independence as its noble mission form the basic character of our Party, a revolutionary Party serving the people.

Our Party was built as a mass party embracing the progressive workers, farmers and working intellectuals in conformity with its intrinsic character as a party serving the people, and has strengthened and developed into a revolutionary party which is rooted deep among the popular masses.

Even when shaping a single policy, our Party, which is infinitely faithful to the people, always goes deep among the people to acquaint itself with their will and demands and mirror them in it. Because they reflect the people's will and demands, all the policies of our Party have become the concern of the popular masses themselves and are applied in their actual lives. In the future, too, we should regard the protection of the people's interests as the supreme principle governing our Party's activities and should ensure that all its activities are conducted fully in keeping with the will and demands of the masses.

If the working-class party is to carry out its mission of serving the people, the party itself should be strengthened unceasingly. Even if it regards serving the people as its mission, the party cannot play its role satisfactorily if it fails to build itself up.

The source of the might of the revolutionary party of the working class lies in its achieving its complete unity and solidarity on the basis of one ideology. Our Party has made its basic line in Party building the establishment of a monolithic ideological system and has striven to embody it fully. This has enabled us to establish the leader's ideological system and system of leadership throughout the party and achieve unbreakable unity and cohesion and, on this basis, to step up the revolution and construction forcefully.

Ensuring continuation in building the working-class party is the guarantee of its invincibility. This is a requirement of the law that guides the development of the communist movement and the party. The revolutionary cause of the working class has to be carried out over a long period of time from generation to generation and the generations change constantly in the course of the development of the communist movement. This makes it necessary for the building of the working-class party to be carried forward and developed through the generations. Ensuring continuation in party building is, in the final analysis, the question of ensuring continuation in party's leadership. The question of the continuation of party leadership for carrying forward the cause of the leader, the pioneer of the revolution, has been solved in our country. In order to ensure continuation in the building of the working-class party, the revolutionary traditions of the party should be protected and revolutionary principles firmly maintained. Socialism develops unceasingly and many problems requiring fresh solutions occur during the advance. However, in the whole process from its beginning to its accomplishment, socialism advances through the course of inheriting, developing and enriching the exploits performed and the experience gained previously. In the course of overcoming grim trials under the guidance of the party and the leader, valuable traditions that will be regarded as a permanent model in the revolution and construction are built up and the principles to be consistently held fast to are established. Our Party has not only solved the problem of the continuation of the leadership but also fully protected and maintained the glorious revolutionary traditions established in the flames of the anti-Japanese revolutionary struggle. It has also consistently adhered to Juche revolutionary lines and policies, and thereby carried the revolutionary cause of Juche unfailingly along the road to victory.

Revolutionary organization and discipline are the life-blood and the source of strength of the working-class party. It leads the revolutionary struggle and construction work, surmounting every manner of trial and difficulty in the fierce class struggle. If it becomes an amorphous body, it cannot work effectively. Our Party embodies the principle of democratic centralism and has firmly established the revolutionary habit of leading a Party life among its members based on the unified rules of a Party life. As a result, it has strengthened and developed into an invincible militant Party with strong organization and discipline, all the members of which act as one under the leader's unitary leadership.

The working-class party should make the basis of its activity work with people. Man is the driving force of the revolution and construction. Accordingly, the working-class party should, through organizational and political work with people, solve all the problems arising in party building and activity. Whether the working-class party discharges its mission to the full or not depends on how it works with people. Our Party has steadfastly converted Party work into work with people, that is, work with cadres, work with Party members and work with the masses, and established a well-regulated system for working with cadres, for guiding Party life and for working with the masses. This has enabled our Party to build itself up strongly and its revolutionary ranks up organizationally and ideologically, as well as to strengthen the driving force of the revolution considerably and, on the basis of this, to promote the revolution and construction.

We should continue to embody the Juche theory on Party building thoroughly and strengthen and develop our Party into a militant political organization which is united on the basis of the monolithic ideological system and which is strong

40

in organization and discipline, into a seasoned political General Staff which at all times ensures its political leadership over society through work with people and into a revolutionary party of a Juche type which invariably defends its revolutionary character.

If the working-class party is to serve the popular masses faithfully in conformity with its intrinsic nature, officials should learn a correct work method and style. However correct party policy may be, it cannot enjoy the support of the people nor be implemented fully if officials are at fault in their work method and style. Only by establishing the revolutionary method and popular style of work that are suited to the nature of socialist society can the trust of the people in the party grow and their revolutionary enthusiasm and creative activity be displayed at a high level in the revolution and construction.

One important problem in establishing a work method and style that are suited to the nature of a socialist society is to overcome the abuse of power and bureaucracy. Being domineering and practicing bureaucracy are an old work method and style which allow officials to wield power by abusing their authority and to behave contrary to the will and interests of the popular masses. Putting an end to the abuse of power and bureaucracy among officials is a vital demand for strengthening the close ties of kinship between the working-class party and the popular masses. The inclination may appear among some officials after the working-class party takes power to try to solve all problems by wielding their power and being domineering and practising bureaucracy. The wielding of power and bureaucracy have nothing in common with the true nature of the working-class party. These are the method of government employed by the reactionary ruling class of the old society. The appearance of such a method in socialist society is mainly due to outmoded ideological remnants in the minds of officials. The work method and style peculiar to the working-class party which struggles for the interests of the people are the revolutionary method and popular style of work. From the first days of building a new society we have set an important task for the Party and state to be to oppose the wielding of power and bureaucracy and to establish the revolutionary method and popular style of work among officials, and we have striven for this. Taking into consideration the fact that the generations change and the number of officials who lack sufficient revolutionary training is on the increase among cadres, we have at all times considered the establishment of the proper method and style of work to be an important task.

In order to put an end to the abuse of power and bureaucracy and to establish the revolutionary method and popular style of work all officials should acquire the habit of serving the popular masses faithfully with the spirit of selfless service for them. This spirit is based on the revolutionary view on the popular masses. This view considers the popular masses to be the masters of the revolution and construction and the most precious and powerful of beings. The revolution and construction are work for the people and work to be done by the people themselves. The popular masses have inexhaustible wisdom and strength. Officials should regard the popular masses as the masters of everything and as the most powerful of beings, respect and love them, believe in their inexhaustible strength and work by relying on it. They should not fall prey to subjectivism or arbitrariness but always lend an ear to the voices of the masses and bring their revolutionary enthusiasm and creative initiative into full play.

Officials are not special beings standing over the masses but their servants who have come from among the masses and serve them. As the servants of the people, officials should always think more of the interests of the people than of their own interests. They should regard the demands and sufferings of the people as their own and help them promptly to solve any difficult problems in their lives and share life and death, good times and bad, with them.

Officials should treat all the people kindly and respect their personality, displaying profound humanity and heart-warming hospitality for them. They should value the socio-political integrity of the people, solve any problems in their socio-political life promptly and treat them without discrimination.

Officials should not be estranged from the popular masses but be on familiar terms with them. They should not put on airs and show off their authority but always be modest and simple in their behaviour. They should not pursue their own interests and seek special favours and preferential treatment, but lead an upright and clean life. They should observe the legal provisions of the state willingly and set examples for the masses in doing difficult and arduous work.

The most worthy way for officials to live is to enjoy the affection and trust of the people while serving them. Faithful to the slogan of the Party, "We serve the people!", they should have a correct view of the popular masses, thoroughly defend the interests of the people and dedicate their all to them.

In order to put an end to the abuse of power and bureaucracy and to establish the revolutionary method and popular style of work a proper work system should be set up. Without going among the masses, officials cannot listen to their voices or work in keeping with their will and demands, nor can they organize and mobilize them. Our Party put forward the slogan, "Let the whole Party go among the masses!" and established a well-organized work system under which all officials go among the masses.

Going among the masses to work has become the habit of our officials and in the course of this subjectivism, bureaucracy, formalism and other outdated work methods and styles have been overcome.

Our Party has ensured that officials not only go among the masses but also keep political work ahead of all other work and solve problems by a political method. Keeping political work ahead of all other work is the intrinsic demand of a socialist society which develops due to the high revolutionary enthusiasm and creative activity of the working people. Our Party put up the slogan, "Let the whole Party become a propagandist and agitator!" and has made sure that all officials go among the masses and give priority to political work to fire the revolutionary enthusiasm of the working people. Our officials go among the masses and arouse them vigorously to join the revolution and construction while explaining Party policies to them and sharing weal and woe with them.

In order to put an end to the misuse of power and bureaucracy and to establish the revolutionary method and popular style of work, ideological education and the ideological struggle should be undertaken boldly by officials. The wielding of power, bureaucracy and the other obsolete work methods and styles are a manifestation of outdated ideological remnants, and they are deep rooted. Without constant ideological education and a continuous ideological struggle among officials it is impossible to eliminate outdated work methods and styles such as the misuse of power and bureaucracy. While ensuring that officials equip themselves fully with the theory and method of Juche leadership created by the great leader, our Party has seen to it that ideological education was provided and an ideological struggle launched with data on positive and negative phenomena manifested in work methods and styles. In the course of persistent ideological education and a continual ideological struggle the wielding of power, bureaucracy and other outdated work methods and styles are being eliminated. As a consequence, the revolutionary method and popular style of work are being firmly established within our Party.

In the future, too, we should continue with the struggle to overcome every manner of outdated work method and style, such as the wielding of power and bureaucracy, and to establish the revolutionary method and popular style of work. In this way we shall strengthen and develop our Party into an invincible revolutionary party which is in perfect harmony with the popular masses and enjoys their unreserved support and confidence, and lead them to accomplish the revolutionary cause of Juche.

Today our people have infinite trust in the Party and the leader and are marching forward along the road indicated by the Party and the leader. Faithful to the slogan, "When the Party is determined, we can do anything!" our people are striving to implement Party lines and policies, through thick and thin. The Party and the leader believe in and have profound love for the people, and the people place absolute trust in the Party and the leader and support them. This is the true nature of our single-hearted unity. Nothing can break the might of our style of socialism in which the leader, the Party and the masses are united as one. By drawing on the might of the single-hearted unity among the leader, the Party and the masses, we must frustrate the anti-socialist machinations of the imperialists and reactionaries, achieve the independent reunification of the country and win without fail the final victory of socialism and communism.

Lightning Source UK Ltd.
Milton Keynes UK
UKOW051809120112

185265UK00002B/100/A